Feathered Friends

Written by Jo Windsor
Illustrated by Richard Hoit

The old man
looked out of the window.
The snow was on the ground.
The snow was on the trees.
"It is cold!" said the old man.

The old man went
into the garden.
He looked at the trees.
He looked at the birds.
"The birds are cold
and hungry," he said.

The old man went
into the house.
"I will make some dinner
for the birds," he said.

The old man
made some dinner
for the birds with:

fat

seeds

and honey.

9

He put the dinner
in a bowl.
"Good!" said the old man.
"The dinner is ready.
The birds will like
this dinner."

The old man went
into the garden.
The birds looked at the old man.
"Come and get your dinner!"
he said.

Up, up, up went the birds.
Up to the dinner.
The old man smiled.
"The birds **love** my dinner!"
he said.

A Menu

BIRD'S MENU

seeds

worms

spiders

apples

snails

Guide Notes

> **Title: Feathered Friends**
> **Stage:** Early (2) – Yellow
>
> **Genre:** Fiction
> **Approach:** Guided Reading
> **Processes:** Thinking Critically, Exploring Language, Processing Information
> **Written and Visual Focus:** Menu
> **Word Count:** 147

THINKING CRITICALLY
(sample questions)

- What do you think this story could be about?
- Discuss the title and ask what this could mean the story is about?
- What time of year do you think this is? How do you know?
- Look at pages 4-5. How do you think the old man feels about the birds?
- If you were going to make this dinner for the birds, what else could you put in?
- Why do you think the birds were pleased with the old man's dinner?

Exploring Language

Terminology
Title, cover, illustrations, author, illustrator

Vocabulary
Interest words: seeds, honey, plate
High-frequency words (reinforced): the, was, is, said, went, at, are, and, will, some, for, with, put, like, this, get, my
New words: ready, made
Positional words: out, into, up, on

Print Conventions
Capital letters for sentence beginnings, full stops, exclamation marks, quotation marks, commas